DATE DUE

WEEKLY WR READER®
EARLY LEARNING LIBRARY

+ SAFETY / LA SEGURIDAD
FIRST / ES LO PRIMERO

Staying Safe / La seguridad
On the Street / en la calle

by/por Joanne Mattern

Reading consultant/Consultora de lectura: Susan Nations, M.Ed.,
author, literacy coach, consultant in literacy development/
autora, tutora de alfabetización, consultora de desarrollo de la lectura

Please visit our web site at: www.garethstevens.com
For a free color catalog describing Weekly Reader® Early Learning Library's list
of high-quality books, call 1-877-445-5824 (USA) or 1-800-387-3178 (Canada).
Weekly Reader® Early Learning Library's fax: (414) 336-0164.

Library of Congress Cataloging-in-Publication Data

Mattern, Joanne, 1963-
   [Staying safe on the street. English & Spanish]
   Staying safe on the street = La seguridad en la calle / by Joanne Mattern.
     p. cm. — (Safety first = La seguridad es lo primero)
   Includes bibliographical references and index.
   ISBN-13: 978-0-8368-8061-8 (lib. bdg.)
   ISBN-13: 978-0-8368-8068-7 (softcover)
   1. Safety education—Juvenile literature. 2. Traffic safety and children—
Juvenile literature. 3. Accidents—Prevention—Juvenile literature. I. Title.
II. Title: Seguridad en la calle.
   HQ770.7.M334   2007b
   363.12'5083—dc22   2006035350

This edition first published in 2007 by
Weekly Reader® Early Learning Library
A Member of the WRC Media Family of Companies
330 West Olive Street, Suite 100
Milwaukee, WI 53212 USA

Copyright © 2007 by Weekly Reader® Early Learning Library

Managing editor: Valerie J. Weber
Editor: Barbara Kiely Miller
Art direction: Tammy West
Cover design and page layout: Charlie Dahl
Picture research: Diane Laska-Swanke
Photographer: Jack Long
Spanish translation: Tatiana Acosta and Guillermo Gutiérrez

The publisher thanks Brandon, Joshua, and Jennifer Turner; Tayler Kozelek; Officer Joel Dhein, Glendale Police
Department; Clifford Karau, Arcade Entertainment; Richard Swanke; and David West for their assistance with
this book.

Printed in the United States of America

1 2 3 4 5 6 7 8 9 10 10 09 08 07 06

Note to Educators and Parents

Reading is such an exciting adventure for young children! They are beginning to integrate their oral language skills with written language. To encourage children along the path to early literacy, books must be colorful, engaging, and interesting; they should invite the young reader to explore both the print and the pictures.

The *Safety First* series is designed to help young readers review basic safety rules, learn new vocabulary, and strengthen their reading comprehension. In simple, easy-to-read language, each book teaches children to stay safe in an everyday situation such as at home, school, or in the outside world.

Each book is specially designed to support the young reader in the reading process. The familiar topics are appealing to young children and invite them to read — and reread — again and again. The full-color photographs and enhanced text further support the student during the reading process.

In addition to serving as wonderful picture books in schools, libraries, homes, and other places where children learn to love reading, these books are specifically intended to be read within an instructional guided reading group. This small group setting allows beginning readers to work with a fluent adult model as they make meaning from the text. After children develop fluency with the text and content, the book can be read independently. Children and adults alike will find these books supportive, engaging, and fun!

— Susan Nations, M.Ed., author/literacy coach/
and consultant in literacy development

Nota para los maestros y los padres

¡Leer es una aventura tan emocionante para los niños pequeños! A esta edad están comenzando a integrar su manejo del lenguaje oral con el lenguaje escrito. Para animar a los niños en el camino de la lectura incipiente, los libros deben ser coloridos, estimulantes e interesantes; deben invitar a los jóvenes lectores a explorar la letra impresa y las ilustraciones.

La seguridad es lo primero es una nueva colección diseñada para ayudar a los jóvenes lectores a repasar normas de seguridad básicas, aprender vocabulario nuevo y reforzar su comprensión de la lectura. Con un lenguaje sencillo y fácil de leer, cada libro enseña a los niños cómo estar seguros en situaciones de la vida diaria en casa, la escuela o cuando salen de paseo.

Cada libro está especialmente diseñado para ayudar a los jóvenes lectores en el proceso de lectura. Los temas familiares llaman la atención de los niños y los invitan a leer una y otra vez. Las fotografías a todo color y el tamaño de la letra ayudan aún más al estudiante en el proceso de lectura.

Además de servir como maravillosos libros ilustrados en escuelas, bibliotecas, hogares y otros lugares donde los niños aprenden a amar la lectura, estos libros han sido especialmente concebidos para ser leídos en un grupo de lectura guiada. Este contexto permite que los lectores incipientes trabajen con un adulto que domina la lectura mientras van determinando el significado del texto. Una vez que los niños dominan el texto y el contenido, el libro puede ser leído de manera independiente. ¡Estos libros les resultarán útiles, estimulantes y divertidos a niños y a adultos por igual!

— Susan Nations, M.Ed., autora/tutora de
alfabetización/consultora de desarrollo de la lectura

You can walk many places. How can you stay safe when you are walking?

- - - - - - - - - - - - - - - -

Podemos ir a muchos sitios caminando. ¿Cómo puedes ir a pie a alguna parte con seguridad?

Stay on the **sidewalk**.

- - - - - - - - - - - - -

Camina por la **acera**.

Certified Public Accountants

sidewalk/acera

7

Never run into the street. Cross at the **corner**.

- - - - - - - - - - - - -

Nunca entres a una calle corriendo. Cruza por la **esquina**.

corner/esquina

9

A **crosswalk** is the best place to cross. Look both ways for cars.

- - - - - - - - - - - - - - - -

Un **paso de peatones** es el mejor lugar para cruzar. Mira a ambos lados para ver si vienen autos.

PUSH
BUTTON
FOR
WALK
SIGNAL

crosswalk/
paso de peatones

11

Do not talk to **strangers**.
Never go with someone
you do not know.

No hables con **extraños**.
Nunca te vayas con personas
desconocidas.

Run away if a stranger tries to give you something. Tell your parents.

Si un extraño trata de darte algo, aléjate corriendo. Avisa a tus padres.

Look for a **police officer** or a fire fighter if you need help.

- - - - - - - - - - - - -

Si necesitas ayuda, busca a un **oficial de policía** o a un bombero.

You can also ask someone who works in a store for help.

También puedes pedirle ayuda a alguien que trabaje en una tienda.

Have fun, but stay safe on the street!

- - - - - - - - - - - - - -

¡Diviértete cuando salgas a la calle, pero no olvides la seguridad!

Glossary

corner — the place where two streets meet

crosswalk — painted lines that show where people should cross the street

police officer — a person whose job is to keep people safe and catch people who break the law

sidewalk — a paved path next to a street

strangers — people you do not know

Glosario

acera — camino pavimentado junto a una calle

esquina — lugar donde se cruzan dos calles

extraños — personas desconocidas

oficial de policía — persona cuyo trabajo consiste en mantener la seguridad y detener a quienes incumplan la ley

paso de peatones — líneas pintadas que indican por dónde se debe cruzar la calle

For More Information/Más información

Books/Libros

A Day with Police Officers. Welcome Books (series). Jan Kottke (Children's Press)

Going to School/De camino a la escuela. My Day at School/Mi dia en la escuela (series). JoAnn Mattern (Gareth Stevens Publishing)

Once Upon a Dragon: Stranger Safety for Kids and Dragons. Jean Pendziwol (Kids Can Press)

¿Quienes nos protegen?/Who Keeps Us Safe? Ellen Catala (Capstone Press)

Señales y rótulos/Signs. David Bauer (Yellow Umbrella Books)

Verde dice adelante/Green Means Go. Susan Ring (Capstone Press)

Index

Índice

About the Author

Joanne Mattern has written more than 150 books for children. She has written about weird animals, sports, world cities, dinosaurs, and many other subjects. Joanne also works in her local library. She lives in New York State with her husband, three daughters, and assorted pets. She enjoys animals, music, going to baseball games, reading, and visiting schools to talk about her books.

Información sobre la autora

Joanne Mattern ha escrito más de ciento cincuenta libros para niños. Ha escrito textos sobre animales extraños, deportes, ciudades del mundo, dinosaurios y muchos otros temas. Además, Joanne trabaja en la biblioteca de su comunidad. Vive en el estado de Nueva York con su esposo, sus tres hijas y varias mascotas. A Joanne le gustan los animales, la música, ir al béisbol, leer y hacer visitas a las escuelas para hablar de sus libros.